The World of HORSES
THOROUGHBREDS

Lorijo Metz

PowerKiDS
press

New York

To Melissa Matson, whose love of all things equine made this book possible

Published in 2013 by The Rosen Publishing Group, Inc.
29 East 21st Street, New York, NY 10010

Editor: Amelie von Zumbusch
Book Design: Kate Laczynski

Photo Credits: Back cover graphic (big horseshoe) © www.iStockphoto.com/Deborah Cheramie; back cover graphic (background horseshoes) Purematterian/Shutterstock.com; cover Irwin Jerry/Photo Researchers/Getty Images; pp. 4–5 Stephen Bonk/Shutterstock.com; pp. 6, 7 (both), 10 iStockphoto/Thinkstock; p. 8 Boston Globe/Contributor/Getty Images; pp. 9, 20, 21 © iStockphoto.com/lillisphotography; p. 11 Design Pics/The Irish Image Collection/Getty Images; pp. 12, 22 Alan Crowhurst/Stringer/Getty Images Sport/Getty Images; p. 13 Mark Dadswell/Staff/Getty Images Sport/Getty Images; p. 14 Rischgitz/Stringer/Hulton Archive/Getty Images; p. 15 Makarova Viktoria (Vikarus)/Shutterstock.com; p. 16 Adam Jones/Photodisc/Getty Images; p. 17 Buyenlarge/Contributor/Archive Photos/Getty Images; p. 18 Heinz Kluetmeier/Contributor/Sports Illustrated/Getty Images; p. 19 Peter Stackpole/Contributor/Time & Life Pictures/Getty Images.

Library of Congress Cataloging-in-Publication Data

Metz, Lorijo.
 Thoroughbreds / by Lorijo Metz. — 1st ed.
   p. cm. — (The world of horses)
 Includes index.
 ISBN 978-1-4488-7429-3 (library binding) — ISBN 978-1-4488-7502-3 (pbk.) —
ISBN 978-1-4488-7576-4 (6-pack)
 1. Thoroughbred horse—Juvenile literature. I. Title.
 SF293.T5M536 2013
 636.1'32—dc23

                                2011051488

Manufactured in China

Contents

Born to Run!

The bell sounds, the gates swing open, and Thoroughbreds burst onto the track! For the next 2 minutes or so, these horses will run as fast as they can. That can mean speeds of over 40 miles per hour (64 km/h)!

The horse's earliest relative, the eohippus, lived 60 million years ago. Thoroughbreds have been

Sometimes Thoroughbreds race on tracks made of dirt, like this one. At other times, they race on turf, or grass.

around for about 300 years. Compared to many other **breeds**, or types of horses, Thoroughbreds are new. Over the centuries, horses have carried people into battle and helped them cross deserts. Other horse breeds have helped people carry heavy loads. Thoroughbreds were **bred**, or raised, to do one thing. That thing is to run fast!

5

People measure horses in hands. One hand equals 4 inches (10 cm). Most Thoroughbreds stand around 16 hands from the ground to the tops of their **withers**, or shoulders. Compared to other breeds, Thoroughbreds are light. They weigh about 1,000 pounds (454 kg). Thoroughbreds have long, powerful legs and short, slim bodies that make them seem even taller.

Thoroughbreds have large, widely spaced eyes.

6

Thoroughbreds come in many colors. The most common colors are brown, gray, chestnut, and bay. Bay horses are reddish brown with black **points**. Points are a horse's mane, tail, and lower legs. Chestnut horses are reddish brown with brown points.

This Thoroughbred is a bay.

Thoroughbreds have small heads and long, graceful necks.

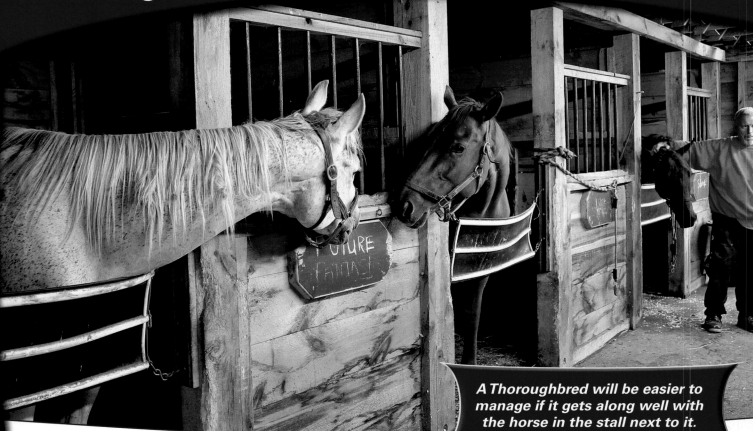

A Thoroughbred will be easier to manage if it gets along well with the horse in the stall next to it.

To stay in top racing form, Thoroughbreds need training and exercise. They also need a stall in a barn or stable. The stall should be filled with fresh straw.

Thoroughbreds eat about 20 pounds (9 kg) of hay every day. They also eat grains, such as oats and barley. They need plenty of fresh water.

Once a day, someone needs to brush their coats and clean their hooves. A Thoroughbred's light horseshoes wear out quickly when racing. When needed, a person called a **farrier** can trim their hooves and replace their horseshoes. A yearly visit from a **veterinarian**, or animal doctor, will help Thoroughbreds stay healthy.

These Thoroughbreds are eating grain. Racehorses tend to eat more grain than horses that are used for other things.

Thoroughbred Foals

Thoroughbred owners choose carefully which horses become parents. They want babies that will grow up to be fast!

Thoroughbred mothers carry their babies for 11 months. Newborns, called **foals**, are born with long legs. They weigh around 110 pounds

More than 100,000 Thoroughbred foals are born each year.

Thoroughbreds can live for 20 to 30 years.

(50 kg). Soon after birth, foals can stand. Within hours, they are running. Foals remain with their mothers for three to six months.

American Thoroughbreds born in the same year are given the same birthday. Whether they are born in February or November, on January 1, they are considered one year old. One-year-old Thoroughbreds are called **yearlings**.

The lines the jockey here is holding are reins. The jockey pulls on them to direct the horse.

Thoroughbreds are hot-blooded, or spirited, horses. This is a great quality to have for bursting onto racetracks. It takes a special person to train Thoroughbreds, though. As yearlings, they learn to follow commands, wear **tack**, and be ridden.

Tack is the special gear horses wear. The saddle and bridle are two pieces of tack. The saddle fits over the horse's back and makes it easier to ride. The bridle fits over the horse's head and is used to control the horse. Thoroughbreds complete their training by learning to race on a racetrack with a **jockey**, or person who rides racehorses.

Thoroughbreds begin racing at around two years old. Most stop racing by five years old.

13

The First Thoroughbreds

The first Thoroughbreds came from England. English people love horse racing. Their horses 300 years ago were big and strong but not very fast. Arabians were the fastest horses. However, they were fairly small and hard to come by.

The Byerley Turk, seen here, belonged to Colonel Robert Byerley.

Between 1680 and 1725, three Arabian **stallions**, or male horses, came to England. The first was from Turkey and known as the Byerley Turk. The second was a reddish-brown horse from Syria known as the Darley Arabian. The third, known as the Godolphin Arabian, was a gift to an English earl.

The English bred these stallions with English **mares**. Their foals were long legged, fast, and strong. They were the first Thoroughbreds!

The first Thoroughbred in North America arrived in 1730. His name was Bulle Rock. His father was the Darley Arabian. People in America loved horse racing. They wanted to raise Thoroughbreds, too. Kentucky became the American center of Thoroughbred

Kentucky is still the center of Thoroughbred breeding in the United States. These Thoroughbreds are on a Kentucky farm.

THE FALSE START — JEROME PARK N.Y.

breeding. It has mild weather and a rich type of grass, called bluegrass.

In England, horse races were 4 miles (6 km) long. Two horses raced at a time. Winners raced other winners until there was one overall winner. Americans wanted shorter, faster races in which all the horses raced at one time. They bred Thoroughbreds that could burst out of the gate and run at full speed from start to finish.

The most famous prize in horse racing is the Triple Crown. To win it, a horse must win three races that take place over a six-week period. These races are the Kentucky Derby, the Preakness Stakes, and the Belmont Stakes. The Triple Crown has been around for over 100 years, but not many horses have won it.

The Kentucky Derby takes place each year on the first Saturday in May.

Two of the most famous Thoroughbreds in history are Man o' War, born in 1917, and Secretariat, born in 1970. Both were chestnut Thoroughbreds. Secretariat won the Triple Crown and went on to set many records. Though Man o' War never won the Triple Crown, he won 20 out of 21 races.

A horse can be registered as a Thoroughbred only if both of its parents were Thoroughbreds.

Registering is a way of labeling a horse so one horse does not race in place of another. England has registered Thoroughbreds since 1831. The Jockey Club registers Thoroughbreds in the United States. All registered Thoroughbreds also have names. Many have both everyday names and special names they use just for racing.

Another way to tell one Thoroughbred from another, whether racing or not, is by its markings. Many Thoroughbreds have white patches of hair on their heads or legs. The special shape of these white markings is one way breeders tell horses apart.

A wide, white stripe down the middle of a horse's face is a blaze. A white mark above or between a horse's eyes is a star.

Thoroughbreds come from a long line of winners. Over 200 years ago, the Thoroughbred Eclipse won every race in which he ran. Eclipse was the great-great-grandson of the Darley Arabian. Almost all Thoroughbreds today are related to Eclipse.

Thoroughbreds do more than race. They compete in horse shows and jumping events. People use them for fox hunting and in polo matches. Thoroughbreds that no longer race often become police horses. These horses have much to offer!

This Thoroughbred is taking part in a steeplechase. This is a race in which horses jump over things, such as walls and hedges.

Glossary

bred (BRED) To have brought a male and a female animal together so they will have babies.

breeds (BREEDZ) Groups of animals that look alike and have the same relatives.

farrier (FER-ee-er) A person who puts shoes on horses.

foals (FOHLZ) Young horses.

jockey (JO-kee) A person who rides racehorses.

mares (MERZ) Adult female horses.

points (POYNTS) A horse's mane, tail, and lower legs.

registering (REH-jih-steh-ring) Putting in an official record book.

stallions (STAL-yunz) Adult male horses.

tack (TAK) The gear used to ride or drive a horse.

veterinarian (veh-tuh-ruh-NER-ee-un) A doctor who treats animals.

withers (WIH-therz) A place between the shoulders of a dog or horse.

yearlings (YIR-lingz) Thoroughbreds during the period that begins January 1 the year after they were born and ends the following January 1.

Index

Websites

Due to the changing nature of Internet links, PowerKids Press has developed an online list of websites related to the subject of this book. This site is updated regularly. Please use this link to access the list:
www.powerkidslinks.com/woh/tho/